T0199080

BRIAN'S
AMAZING
MAZES

Copyright © 2020 by Brian Nunez. 812276

All rights reserved. No part of this book may be
reproduced or transmitted in any form or by
any means, electronic or mechanical, including
photocopying, recording, or by any information
storage and retrieval system, without permission in
writing from the copyright owner.

This is a work of fiction. Names, characters, places
and incidents either are the product of the
author's imagination or are used fictitiously, and
any resemblance to any actual persons, living or
dead, events, or locales is entirely coincidental.

To order additional copies of this book, contact:
Xlibris
1-888-795-4274
www.Xlibris.com
Orders@Xlibris.com

ISBN: Softcover   978-1-9845-8024-5
         Hardcover   978-1-9845-8025-2
         EBook   978-1-9845-8026-9

Print information available on the last page

Rev. date: 05/20/2020

BRIAN'S
AMAZING
MAZES

BRIAN NUNEZ

EXIT

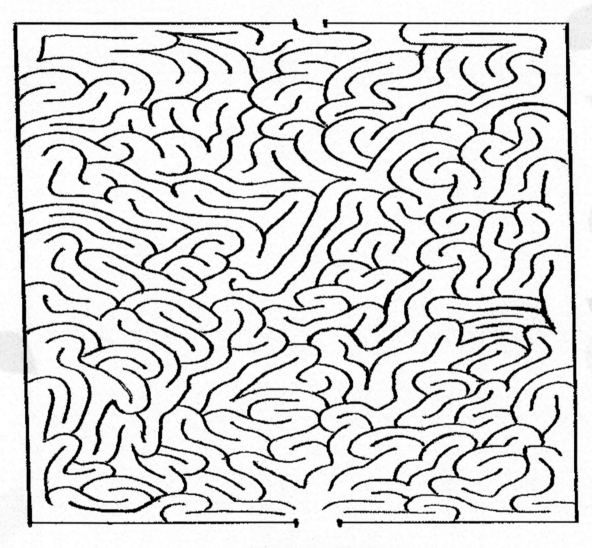

ENTER

EXIT

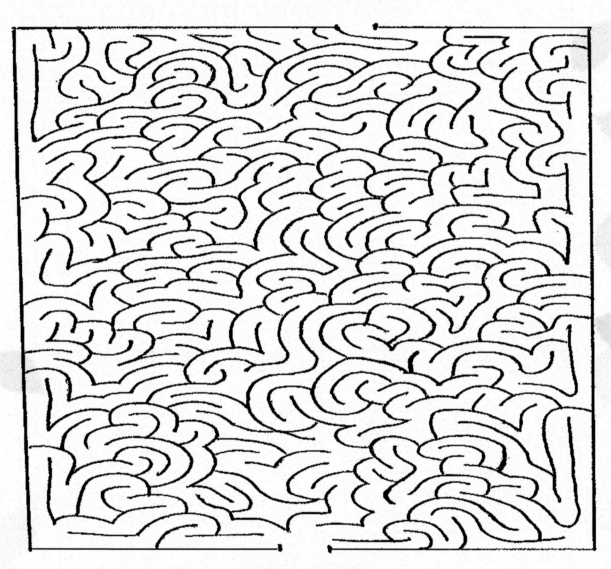

ENTER

EXIT

ENTER

EXIT

ENTER

EXIT

ENTER

EXIT

ENTER

EXIT

ENTER

EXIT

ENTER

EXIT

ENTER

EXIT

ENTER

EXIT

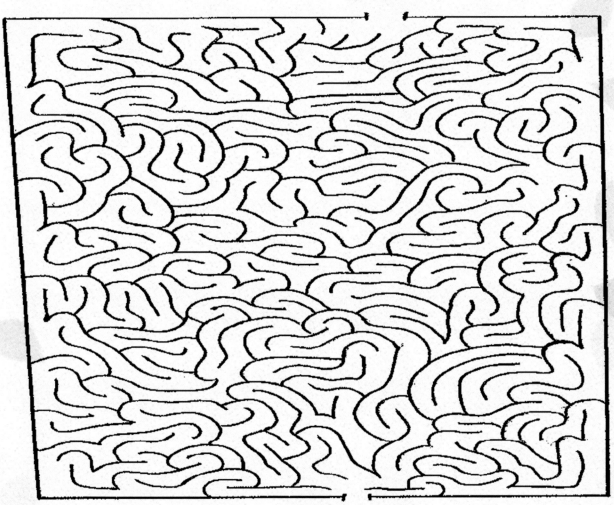

ENTER

EXIT

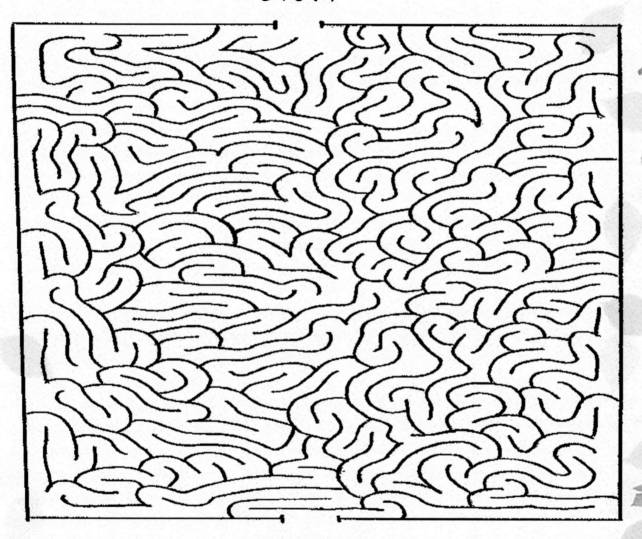

ENTER

EXIT

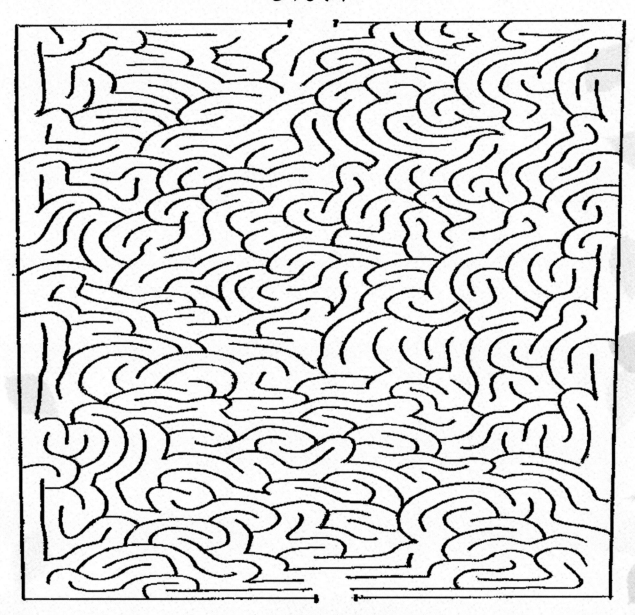

ENTER

EXIT

ENTER

EXIT

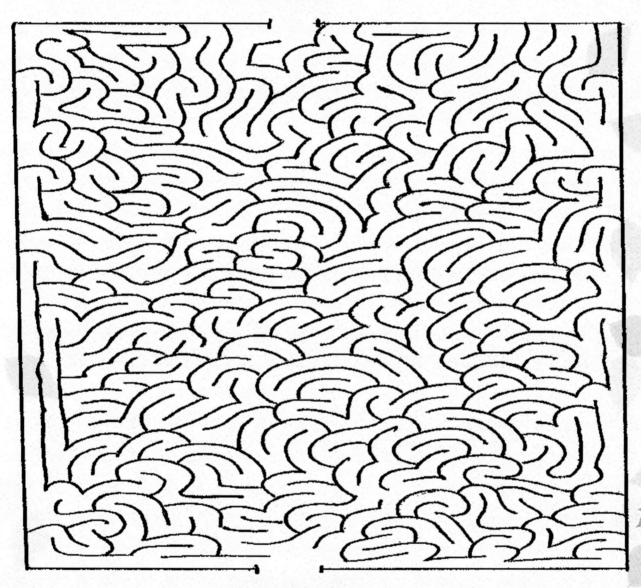

ENTER

EXIT

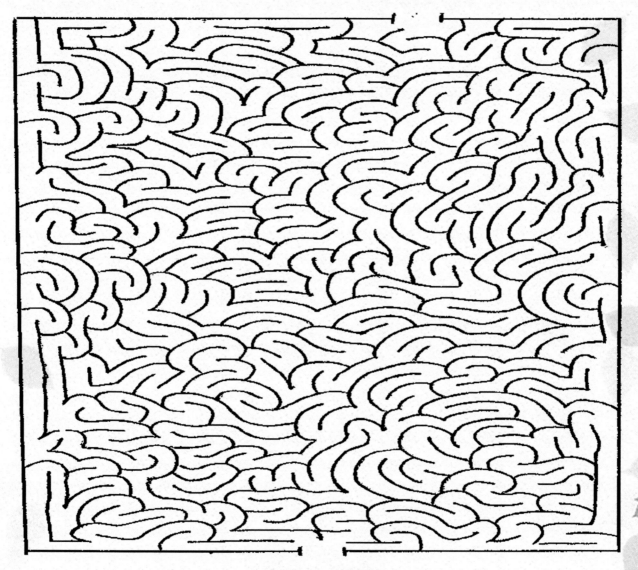

ENTER

EXIT

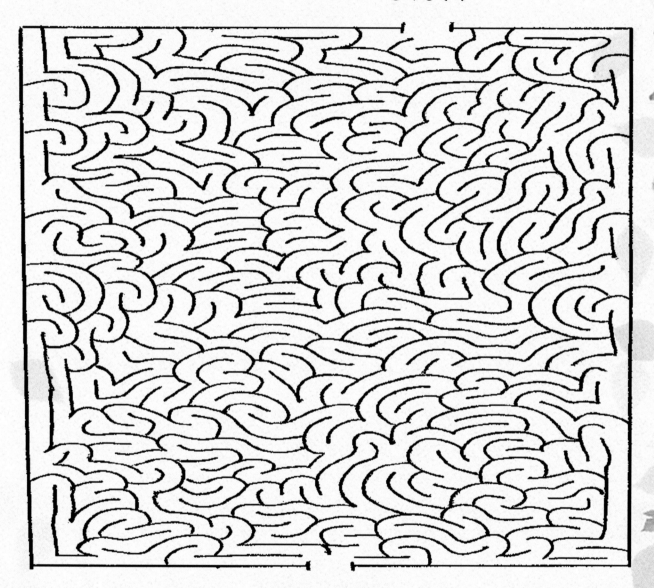

ENTER

EXIT

ENTER

EXIT

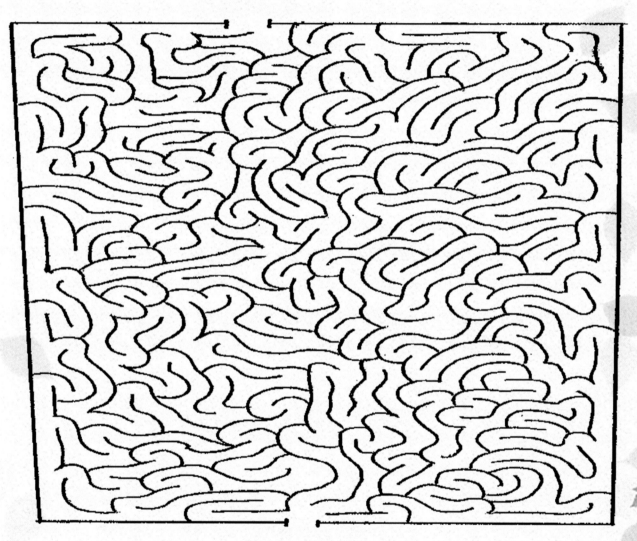

ENTER

EXIT

ENTER

EXIT

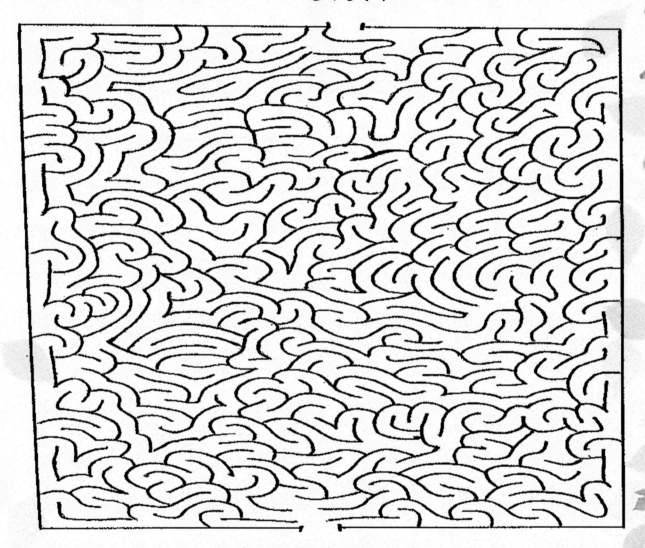

ENTER

EXIT

ENTER

EXIT

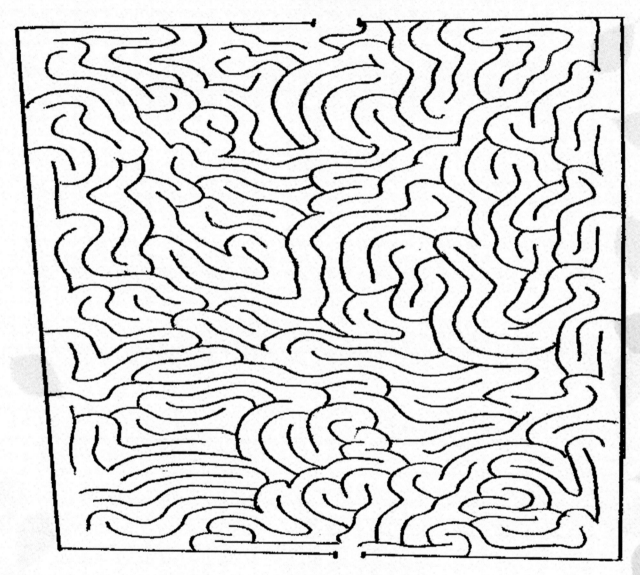

ENTER

EXIT

ENTER

EXIT

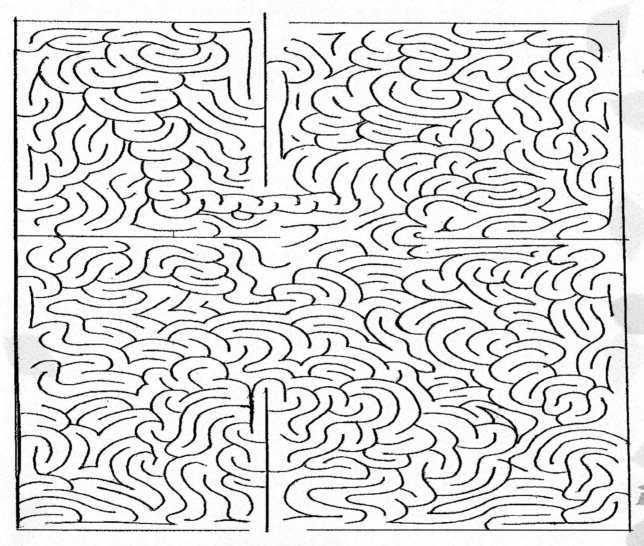

ENTER

EXIT

ENTER

Printed in the United States
By Bookmasters